Ukulele Breakthrough

Ukulele Breakthrough

✦

Helping you go from lonely strummer to life-of-the-party!

Calvin Chin

Richard Woike, editor

iUniverse, Inc.
New York Lincoln Shanghai

Ukulele Breakthrough
Helping you go from lonely strummer to life-of-the-party!

iUniverse, Inc.

For information address:
iUniverse, Inc.
2021 Pine Lake Road, Suite 100
Lincoln, NE 68512
www.iuniverse.com

Note to the reader: I've made every effort to include only ukulele arrangements of songs that are in the Public Domain. If I've inadvertently violated a musical license I apologize and will delete any copyrighted property as soon as possible.

ISBN: 0-595-31258-6

Printed in the United States of America

This book is lovingly

dedicated to Rose.

Contents

INTRO: WHERE YOU ARE—AND WHERE WE'RE GOING

This book is for you if you've tried playing the ukulele, and you want to know how to read and play chords from any sheet music. These lessons include advanced and modified chords that can help make your performances richer and more enjoyable.

Most ukulele books show chord diagrams above the notes. That may be OK for individual songs. But then you've got the almost endless job of memorizing chords.

This book *is* a real breakthrough, because it shows that when you learn about 50 chord shapes you can play literally hundreds of chords—just by sliding your hand up and down the fretboard.

For all the practice songs and examples, tune your uke to the notes G-C-E-A; the old "My Dog Has Fleas" melody.

Look at the 12 frets on your uke, which mark off the 12 notes of a full octave. These note intervals are based on the "RULE OF NONE." The rule applies to the 12 ascending notes of the scale, beginning with the open sound of each string.

For instance, pluck each note on your A-string, starting with the string open. The first note will be an A, of course. The next is a B flat (Bb). Then, moving down[1] one fret at a time, play B, then C, Db, D, Eb, E, F, Gb, G, Ab, and A. That's a complete chromatic scale on the A-string. Its last note is an octave above the open string note. The RULE OF NONE is that there's _no_ note between B and C, nor between E and F. Never. NONE.[2]

---

1.   In this book, "up" refers to frets nearer the nut end of the fretboard. "Down" or "below" refer to the higher-sounding notes near the sound hole. I'll also use "shapes" to mean the chord formations that are movable up and down. "Fingering" refers to suggested positions of your fingers as you form the chords.
2.   Appendix A shows the note sequences for all 12 scales.

Chromatic scale means that there is a note between the other "letter" notes. Just to keep it simple, I'll always refer to those intervals as flats (b). So, to find, say, the Db on the A-string, just move your finger down the frets as you count from Bb to B to C (the RULE OF NONE in action)—to Db.

When you apply the RULE to locate the right fret you won't need charts or diagrams, because the note of the fret tells you the name of the chord you are holding.

Each uke string can be the root of its own set of chords—basic and advanced. For instance, the A-string has its own major, minor, seventh, and other types. So do the other three strings. The lessons ahead show you how to play them all.

By the time you've read (and played through) all the lessons, you'll know how to form over 500 chords. With that many, you can probably play almost every song you've ever wanted to learn. Let's get started!

LESSON 1: BASIC CHORDS ON THE A-STRING

The diagrams over on the right show the shapes of 3 chord types based on the A-string: major, minor, and seventh. For example, to play a Bb major, put your index finger on the Bb fret of the A-string and on the F fret of the E-string. Place your second and third fingers on the other frets. The Bb note here produces the Bb chord root. Incidentally, the column of notes to the right side of each diagram represents the chromatic scale on the darker line representing the A-string.

Now, try the minor and 7th chords, following the diagrams.

Among the examples, note the difference in the shapes of the A major and the A7. Your index finger isn't needed to bar the first fret. The open strings do that for you.

When you've formed a chord shape, hold your fingers in the same position as you slide them up and down the fret board, striving for good clear sound. When you sound halfway decent, you're ready for a little tryout with the music at the end of this lesson.

But wait! Preview the diagramed chord shapes first. You might have to do a little counting up and down the strings. Start strumming the chords in the tune, slowly at first. After a few tries you'll improve gradually.

Play "The Band Played On" and "Meet Me in St. Louis" just with the chords based on the A-string. You'll learn the fret board well by playing these so-called "one string serenades." Trust me!

It's difficult to play a minor chord at the bottom of the fret board, so see the inversion of such a chord with the Minors examples. The Bbm and the Dm are like the original on the top of the page; whereas the inversion (Am) has the ring finger barring 3 strings and the index finger pressing the E note on the G-string. Inversions are interchangeable with the originals. The Gm near the end of "The Band Played On" is a good place for an inversion.

So that's Lesson One: a way to find lots and lots of chords—using just the A-string.

Basic A-string Chords

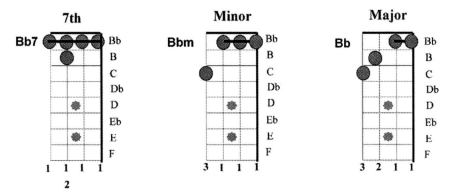

Recommended fingering positions (noted under the fret board illustrations):
1 = Index - 2 = Middle - 3 = Ring - 4 = Pinkie

Some examples:

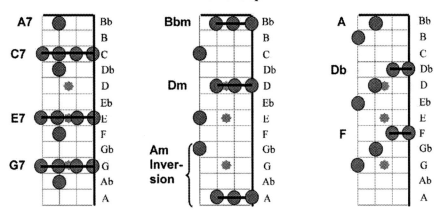

A line connecting two or more notes means that
you should bar across those notes in the chord.

The Band Played On

Charles B. Ward

Arrangement by Calvin Chin

Meet Me in St. Louis

Words by ANDREW STERLING
Music by KERRY MILLS

Arranged by Calvin Chin

LESSON 2: BASIC CHORDS ON THE E-STRING

As you already suspect, you can play all those chords on the E-string, as well. The shapes are different, but it's still better to learn just three shapes at a time than to memorize all 48 chords, no?

Just as in the previous lesson, the three chords on the opposite page are labeled with the numbers of the fingers I suggest that you use for the individual notes. For the Major chord, slide your <u>middle</u> finger down the E-string from the first fret (F) to each succeeding fret until that finger reaches the desired fret. And remember the RULE as you move down from fret to fret. Also, it's very important, as you focus on the E-string, to start at the top and work down to the proper fret. By following this method, you'll gradually absorb *deep* knowledge of the entire fretboard.

For the Minor, place your *ring* finger on the E-string on the top fret and count down to the proper fret to apply the rest of the fingering. Similarly, for the 7th chord—say, Ab7—place your *index* finger on the top fret of the E-string (the F), slide it down to Gb, and then G, then stop on the next fret (Ab), and make the rest of the chord shape to play the Ab7 chord.

Notice the inversion for the E-minor. You can play that chord either way to get the same sound. Sometimes, the fingering of the inversion is easier than the standard shape.

Practice forming the example chords shown on the lower part of the page opposite. When your chords sound good and clear, you're ready to try them on "Cradle Song," and "I Wonder Who's Kissing Her Now." Play these two songs using just chords based on the E-string, to reinforce your memory of these new shapes and fingerings.

The skill you gain by playing difficult chords near the bottom of the keyboard will pay off for you later, with greater versatility and more interesting musical flourish in your improvisations.

Basic E-string Chords

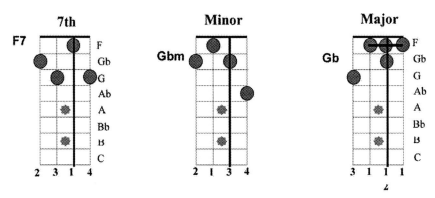

Recommended fingering positions (noted under the fret board illustrations):
1 = Index - 2 = Middle - 3 = Ring - 4 = Pinkie

Some examples:

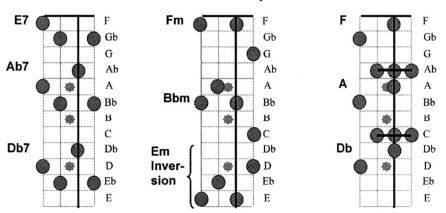

A line connecting two or more notes means that
you should bar across those notes in the chord.

Cradle Song

JOHANNES BRAHMS

Arranged by Calvin Chin

I Wonder Who's Kissing Her Now

Lyrics by HOUGH & ADAMS   Music by JOE HOWARD & HAROLD ORLOB

Arranged by Calvin Chin

LESSON 3: BASIC CHORDS ON THE C-STRING

The numbered fingering on the opposite page shows you how to form another set of chords. Try these shapes, sliding up and down the fretboard. Strum a whole octave of each chord type.

When you're satisfied with your fingering, locate some chords of your own choice, e.g., G, F, Ab.

Use the RULE OF NONE, as usual. Start at the top fret, and then move down along the C-string until you reach the note you want. Then, place the rest of your fingers in the correct positions shown in the diagrams.

The "finding process" is the same for all the strings. All four strings are tuned differently, so you'll learn faster by always starting at the top fret.

When you're satisfied with your fluidity and comfort in playing these chords, try them out on the two songs for this lesson—"Gypsy Love Song" and "Greensleeves," using only chords based on the C-string.

But first, another brief word about inversions. In the example charts, look at the G and A majors. The G chord is the standard shape for the majors based on the C-string. But the A major chord shown here is an inversion. It includes a C (on the A-string), instead of a G. Strum both forms of the A major and listen for the inversion's slightly higher tone quality. To form it, you'll probably need to bar across all the strings with your index finger and use your pinky to hold the note three frets down.

Basic C-string Chords

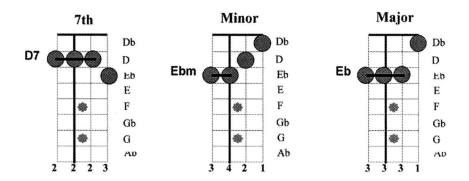

Some examples:

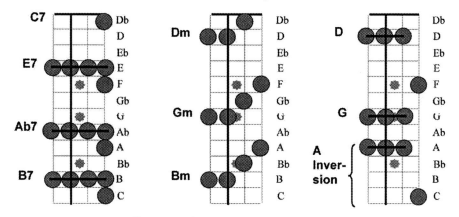

A line connecting two or more notes means that
you should bar across those notes in the chord.

Gypsy Love Song

VICTOR HERBERT

Slum-ber on, my lit-tle gyp-sy sweet-heart, Dream of the field and the grove, ___

Can you hear me, hear me in that dream-land, Where your fan-cies rove?

Slum-ber on, my lit-tle gyp-sy sweet-heart, Wild lit-tle wood-land dove,

Can you hear the song that tells you All my heart's true love? ___

Arranged by Calvin Chin

Greensleeves

English folk song

Arranged by Calvin Chin

LESSON 4: BASIC CHORDS ON THE G-STRING

The major chord shape on the opposite page is difficult, except at the very top of the fretboard (where the G is open). For me, it's almost impossible farther down, so I dispense with it.

However, it's not entirely essential, because you have some easier substitutes along the C, E, and A-strings. You could just play the G major (a nice partly disappearing specimen) as your only major chord based on this string—unless you have very long, supple fingers. Of course, the other cure for stretching difficulty is found in faithful, consistent practice. If you're into the ukulele for the long run, you'll be glad to reach the right chord *anywhere* on the fretboard. Up to you!

As to the 7th and Minor chords, one more time: Get your fingers in the right shape; then put your index finger on the first G-string fret and slide it to the note you want. Eventually, it'll be second nature for you to hit the right spot right away.

Unless you've got the fret names down cold, keep reciting those note names as you go. It certainly doesn't hurt to "play 'em as you say 'em," because that repetitive association all goes into your brain *somewhere*, and it might do you good some day!

And while you're counting, don't forget the RULE.

I should mention at this stage in your progress, that you don't HAVE to do the chord fingering as shown in the diagrams. If a particular fingering is difficult for you, but you have a more convenient way, by all means use it! Remember that the most important thing to achieve is smooth transition from one chord to the next. So, place your fingers however they work best for you, to change chords without stumbling

Okay, try a bunch of these G-string chords, and mix them with previous chords you've learned on the other strings. When you're satisfied with your fingering of these chords, try them on "In the Good Old Summertime" and "Indiana."

Basic G-string Chords

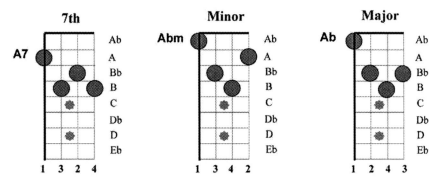

Recommended fingering positions (noted under the fret board illustrations):
1 = Index - 2 = Middle - 3 = Ring - 4 = Pinkie

Some examples:

A line connecting two or more notes means that
you should bar across those notes in the chord.

In the Good Old Summertime

Words by REN SHIELDS
Music by GEORGE EVANS

Arranged by Calvin Chin

Indiana
(Back Home Again in Indiana)

Words by BALLARD MACDONALD
Music by JAMES F. HANLEY

Arranged by Calvin Chin

LESSON 5: TWO DRAMATIC CHORDS *(and more!)*

The diagrams across the page illustrate the finger positions for the diminished and augmented chords that you can use to add some interesting variety to your playing. Their symbols are:

For diminished: **o** (or "dim")

For augmented: **+** (or "aug")

On sheet music, these symbols are written: Dbo, Dbdim, G+, Gaug, and so on. As you try the fingering shapes, you'll see that these chords are pretty easy to hold.

Notice that by moving to just three consecutive positions along the frets, you can play all possible diminished chords. Each of these shapes are four diminished chords *simultaneously*, because of the simple fact that this type of chord contains four notes (unlike the types you've learned in the last 4 lessons, and unlike Augmented chords). And each chord position has four "names," one for each note!

Now, look at the top Augmented examples. This is an A+ (augmented) chord because one of its notes is an A. It's also a Db augmented, because—yes!—it contains a Db. And so on. In other words, if you play a note in this chord shape, that note is one of the chord's three names. What could be easier?

Notice the three Augmented positions inverted, in the right-hand column You can see that only the finger on the A-string changes. Interesting, or not?

Up to this point in the course, I've wanted you to try playing each practice song using only one string as the base for all the chords. But from now on, try to use any chord that fits the song, regardless of its base string. Let tone quality and avoidance of squeakiness be your goal. As you recap all the chord possibilities you've learned, these practice sessions should become more satisfying and fun.

Once you've practiced a little with diminished and augmented chords, try them out on "Aloha Oe" and "Red River Valley."

Two Dramatic Chords
(Diminished & Augmented)

Diminished
Symbol: ° or dim
FIRST POSITION

G° Db° E° Bb°

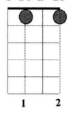

1   2

Augmented
Symbol: + or aug
FIRST POSITION

A+ Db+ F+ A+

2   1   1

Augmented Inversions
Symbol + or aug
FIRST POSITION

Ab+ C+ E+ C+

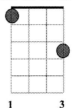

1   3

SECOND POSITION

Ab° D° F° B°

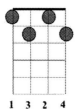

1   3   2   4

SECOND POSITION

Bb+ D+ Gb+ Bb+

3   2   2   1

SECOND POSITION

A+ Db+ F+ Db+

2   1   1   3

THIRD POSITION

A° Eb° Gb° C°

1   3   2   4

THIRD POSITION

B+ Eb+ G+ B+

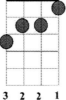

3   2   2   1

THIRD POSITION

Bb+ D+ Gb+ D+

2   1   1   3

Aloha Oe
Farewell to Thee

Words by RAYMOND KLAGES
Music by QUEEN LILIOUKALANI

Arranged by Calvin Chin

Red River Valley

Arranged by Calvin Chin

LESSON 6: A SELF-EXAMINATION ON MIDWAY FRETS

Well, we're about halfway through the first part of this ukulele improvement effort. It's a good time to give yourself a test, to see if you can really use everything you've learned to make decent-sounding music. When you're satisfied, keep on going through the rest of the lessons.

Unless you're a rare genius, you need a lot of practice with the advanced chords, and a lot of time working with and thinking about your fretboard. The more you play actual songs, the sooner you'll be able to easily strum chords that really produce the sounds these composers intended (rather than the compromise sounds you sometimes get from the limited "basic" chords like G, C, F, D7—the stuff you learned from elementary ukulele books).

Since the ukulele is so much fun to play, though, your practicing should be a pleasure. Just remember that by the time you slug all the way through these lessons with an hour or so of practice every day, you'll be able to play many all-time great songs.

Also, the point of knowing all the chord shapes on every string is that you can play more efficiently—using chords close together, instead of making your hand race to far-away frets. Sliding up or down very far when you're playing fast, you're likely to make more mistakes. And it's more stressful. But...the uke is *supposed* to be a stress-reducing instrument!

Not only will your use of midway chords exercise your knowledge up to this point. They also give you the opportunity to use different fingering and produce higher tones than chords at the top of the fretboard. Besides, playing chords in closer proximity lets you slide more melodiously from one to another and make smoother transitions.

There's another reason you should try playing more midway chords: the possibility of added emphasis. You've already learned that diminished and augmented chords can produce tones that add drama to your rendition, especially when you do more emphatic strumming. Playing chords in the midway fret range is another way to introduce variety and color.

As you've learned, the four different fingerings available for every chord type give you greater ability to add expressiveness and the unique touch of your own personality. And by moving further down the fretboard you have more creative tools for interpreting each song you play. So, use the midway chords to achieve a higher pitch, to produce more interesting chord progression, and to have more pleasing and melodic endings.

Playing only the top frets doesn't do much to help you learn the whole fretboard. It constrains the variety the ukulele can give you. There is good reason, after all, that your instrument spans the range of tones (at least an octave) on each string. So...fire up your imagination and experiment with your new-found knowledge.

As you study the music for a song, make your own notations to mark the places where midway chords could be used to good effect. Draw a line under each chord you think might sound better with more emphasis or higher pitch. Use an arrow to indicate where to slide into the next chord.

Just to let you demonstrate that you can play all the chord types you've learned so far on every string, here's your self-test. As you go along, you'll know exactly how well you're doing.

THE TEST: Play the songs of Lessons 1 through 5; but this time, play all the chords within a 5-fret span, either Frets 3 through 7, or 4 through 8. This keeps you in the area midway down the neck of your instrument—home of the "Midway Chords."

Play whatever chords are in these songs—the Majors, the Minors, the 7ths, and the Augmented and Diminished. When you decide which string you'll base a chord on, consider how close it is to the previous chord. Often, you'll only have to slide a couple of frets. This means that you must look for the key note to base the chord on, and that note could be just a fret or two away from the current fingering or chord.

Don't get discouraged if this exercise forces you to play slower. Don't even think about the rhythm for a while, until you're comfortable finding chords that are close to each other. The speed comes with practice. But you knew *that!*

This is a great test of better ukulele playing. How are you doing?

LESSON 7: ADVANCED A-STRING CHORDS

The diagrams across the page give you the finger positions of four advanced chords for the A-string: the Minor 7ths, Sixths, Minor 6ths, and Ninths.

It's pretty obvious that this isn't a book about music theory, but with these Ninth chords, it's helpful to understand a little more about the structure of the scale. The ninth chord is unique, because it's the only one that requires a note two frets above the note that names the chord.

Actually, the Ninth chord is just a Seventh with a ninth note added. As you see in the examples of the Ninths, the Db9 needs you to play the note two frets down from Db, so your ring finger is on the Eb. Again, the main diagram for Ninths shows that you play the Bb9 by placing your ring finger two frets down the fretboard from Bb; and that would be the C.

Another way to look at it: the "Ninth" refers to the note that's two notes above the given (chord-name) note. So, in a scale of 7 major notes—say, from A to G and then continuing through the cycle again—we'd find that A is both the first and the eighth note. Similarly, if the given chord is the C9, its first and eighth note are C's. Therefore, two higher frets are added to the C7 to get the C9. Thanks to the wonderful consistency of music, the same formula applies to the other notes, as well.

For further clarification, look at Appendix A ("Chords By The Numbers")

As for the Minor 6ths, 6ths, and Minor 7ths, practice as usual, and try again to use the fingering in the diagrams

Play the whole range of 12 chords for each of these chord shapes on the A-string. By now, you should have your learning routine down pat. Just spend a few minutes running up and down the fretboard, and playing a whole octave of each chord shape.

After you've played all these advanced chords and are satisfied with your progress, try them out on "Smiles" and "Some of These Days".

Advanced A-string Chords

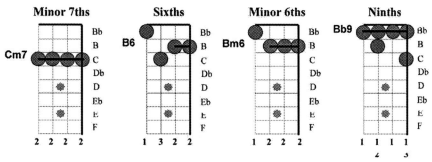

Recommended fingering positions (noted under the fret board illustrations):
1 = Index - 2 = Middle - 3 = Ring - 4 = Pinkie

Some examples:

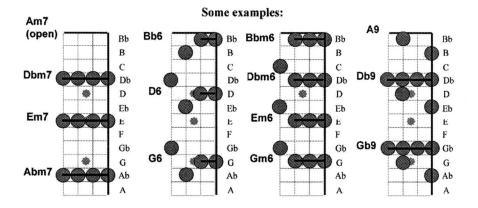

A line connecting two or more notes means that
you should bar across those notes in the chord.

Smiles

Words by J. WILL CALLAHAN
Music by LEE S. ROBERTS

Arranged by Calvin Chin

Some of These Days

Arranged by Calvin Chin

LESSON 8: ADVANCED E-STRING CHORDS

Well, by this time you certainly know what to look for and what to do with the lesson diagrams.

Note that the fret you press on the E-string gives its name to the Minor 6, Sixth, and Minor 7th chords. But, as you learned in the last lesson, the Ninths include a note *two* notes higher than the note indicated by the chord name.

You might also notice an interesting coincidence in some of the chord shapes. The shape of the E-string Ninth is the same as the shape of the A-string Minor 6ths. And the A-string Ninths' shape is the same as the E-string Minor Sixths. Strange but true!

Seeing that little symmetry may help you remember the fingering.

Or maybe not.

The best way to get your fingering fast and tight and smooth is to *practice and play—at least an hour a day.* Believe it!

As you play the old favorites "My Wild Irish Rose" and "I'm Always Chasing Rainbows," try to combine advanced chords from both the A and E strings, when you need these more sophisticated sounds. Remember to keep making your choices based on where you can make the smallest or easiest changes, using chords you've learned in all the lessons so far.

If you've learned most of everything up to here, you've really got it made, because you're playing the uke better than you ever did before. And it should be a lot easier for the rest of the way. Believe it…and Enjoy it!

Advanced E-string Chords

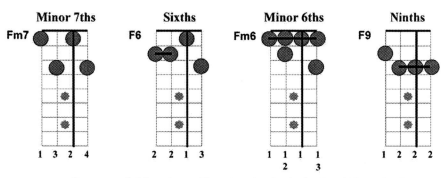

Recommended fingering positions (noted under the fret board illustrations):
1 = Index - 2 = Middle - 3 = Ring - 4 = Pinkie

Some examples:

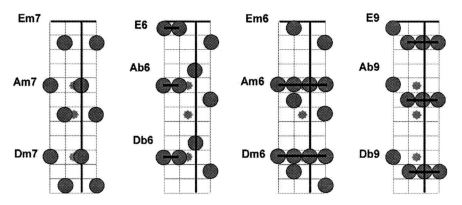

A line connecting two or more notes means that
you should bar across those notes in the chord.

My Wild Irish Rose

By CHAUNCEY OLCOTT

Arranged by Calvin Chin

I'm Always Chasing Rainbows

Music by HARRY CARROLL
Lyrics by JOSEPH McCARTHY

Arranged by Calvin Chin

LESSON 9: ADVANCED C-STRING CHORDS

Again, you've got a series of chord shape diagrams to work with on a single string.

Remember—from the last two lessons—that each Ninth chord includes a note two frets above the note that names the chord.

As you've done before, finger each chord along the whole range of frets of the C-string, working with these diagrams and examples.

Then, as you play "When You Were Sweet Sixteen" and the "Ave Maria," try to combine advanced chords from the A-, E-, and C-strings. And keep working to develop the habit of choosing the base string for your chords that will mean the smallest moves up and down the fretboard.

Also practice these songs while using the Midway chords, starting on the 3rd or 4th frets. As you play, pay attention to the individual notes you're playing with each finger. You'll see that when you play A-string chords the notes C and D are under the fingers of your left hand. On E-string chords you'll find G and A. On C-string chords, they are near Eb, E, and F and on the G-string will be close to Bb, B, and C. As you use midway chords on these strings, then, you'll have the roots for all possible chords right under your left hand. Take advantage of these proximities to play without moving very much at all!

Advanced C-string Chords

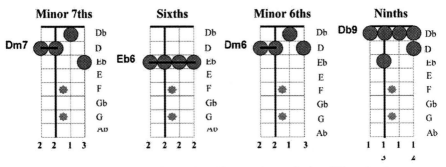

Recommended fingering positions (noted under the fret board illustrations):
1 = Index   -   2 = Middle   -   3 = Ring   -   4 = Pinkie

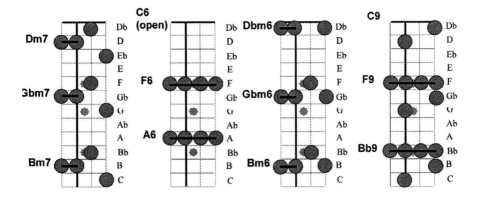

A line connecting two or more notes means that
you should bar across those notes in the chord.

When You Were Sweet Sixteen

By JAMES THORNTON

Arranged by Calvin Chin

Ave Maria

BACH - GOUNOD

Arranged by Calvin Chin

LESSON 10: ADVANCED G-STRING CHORDS

Well, you should know how to learn these new chords: the Minor 7ths, Sixths, Minor 6's and Ninths based on the G-string.

As you check out the "Note that names the chord," notice again how the Ninths require that a higher (by two frets) note must be played on the same string as the chord-name note. When you remember that, it'll help you recall the shape of all the Ninths.

You should also notice, if you haven't already, that some chord shapes are identical. Don't let that confuse you! Depending on the base string of the chord, the same shape can give you a Minor 7th (if played on the A-string) and a Sixth (on the C). A Ninth on the G-string looks just like a Minor 6 on the C.

This is mildly interesting, no? It might also help you remember the shapes.

Speaking of remembering, you might recall that in Lesson 4 I mentioned that the G-string majors are difficult for most people to play. I hope that you've been diligent in practicing them anyway, because if you can play the basic G's, it'll help you now. If you weren't diligent before, it's never too late!

Also, still on the subject of practice, I urge you to keep doing practice drills using the midway frets. Just limit yourself to any 5-fret span and play all the chord types you've learned, starting with the A-string. Recite their names as you play them, and you'll reinforce your memory.

When you've practiced the advanced G-string chords to your own satisfaction, try them in those great old sentimental favorites, "I Love You Truly" and "In the Shade of the Old Apple Tree." First play the advanced chords just based on the G-string for a couple of times through the songs. Then, use any chords that will keep your moves up and down the fretboard as short as possible.

And relax—this is *supposed* to be enjoyable!

Advanced G-string Chords

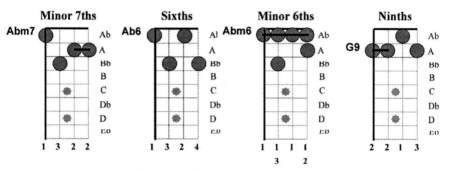

Recommended fingering positions (noted under the fret board illustrations):
1 = Index - 2 = Middle - 3 = Ring - 4 = Pinkie

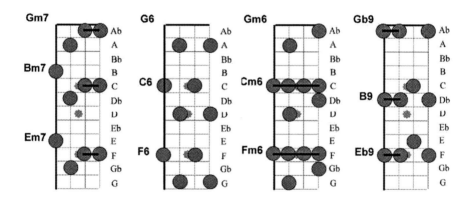

A line connecting two or more notes means that
you should bar across those notes in the chord.

I Love You Truly

CARRIE JACOBS BOND

Arranged by Calvin Chin

In the Shade of the Old Apple Tree

Words by HARRY M. WILLIAMS
Music by EGBERT VAN ALSTYNE

Arranged by Calvin Chin

LESSON 11: The Exotic Major 7ths

The Major 7th chords (not to be confused with the plain old 7ths 'way back in the first lesson) are the last type of chords I'll describe that have names. After this lesson, the chords in the book will be unnamed, believe it or not.

I call these Major 7ths "exotic" because you'll often find them in difficult pieces of music, and frankly, they can be pretty challenging to play. Also, they can sometimes sound as if they're out of tune. But they do produce very precise tones that fall subtly in between some of the more conventional chords. When you become comfortable with Major 7ths, try to use them as improv chords in some of your favorite songs.

The hardest string to base Major 7ths on is the E, without a doubt. Fortunately, as you know, if the E-string shape is impossible for *your* hand there are still three strings' worth of alternatives.

Here's a good place for an inverted chord: when you play the FM7 based on the E-string, you can play it just by lifting your Ring Finger (#3) from the diagramed shape. That's an example of how an inversion can be easier than the "regular" shape. Remember, though, you'll do yourself a favor by being able to play each of these chords both ways: regular and inverted. However, only the FM7 could be so easy.

You can try out these strange-and-different and very sophisticated chords on "Give My Regards to Broadway" and on the old romantic favorite "Because."

Exotic Chords: the Major 7ths

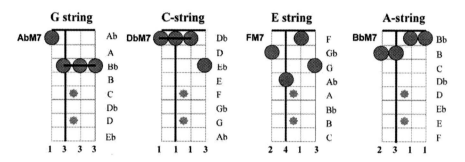

Recommended fingering positions (noted under the fret board illustrations):
1 = Index - 2 = Middle - 3 = Ring - 4 = Pinkie
NOTE: Major 7th chord names are indicated with a capital "M"

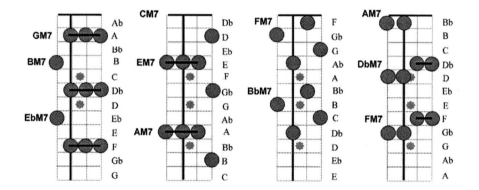

A line connecting two or more notes means that
you should bar across those notes in the chord.

Give My Regards To Broadway

GEORGE M. COHAN

Arranged by Calvin Chin

Because

GUY D'HARDELOT

Arranged by Calvin Chin

LESSON 12: 7th CHORDS WITH RAISED OR LOWERED 5ths

These aren't really chord names as much as they are descriptions. The chords are a bit different than those we've used earlier, because you can play 'em each two ways.

The chord shapes you'll learn in this lesson can give you some nice tonal shadings. When you try them, compare them with the "regular" 7ths.

They're all based on the 7ths you've been using as long as you've played the uke. The variations here are that they can be notated as "+5" or "-5" (or sometimes as # or b). And that means you change the note on one string.

Look at the chord shapes on the next page. The first example—Ab7+/-5—shows two dotted circles for the fret changes to play these chords. Beginning with a "standard" 7th based on the G-string, the string on which the note changes is always next to the chord-naming ("root") string *on the same side of the fretboard*. Here's a table to help you remember this rule:

Root String	Change String
G	C
C	G
E	A
A	E

The change is always one fret up or below the "regular" 5th note.

Look at the examples in the lower left, of Bb7+5 and Bb7-5, based on the G-string root. The +5 variation includes Bb, Gb, Ab, and D. To change from +5 to -5, you lower the C string note two frets. In this case that would be from Gb down the scale to E. (Remember, according to the old RULE OF NONE, that the two notes down from Gb are F, and then E.). So, the -5 variation includes Bb, E, Ab, and D.

In the first C-string example (Db7 +/- 5), this chord is one of the "partly-disappearing" variety. The G-string note you play is an A (for +5) or down two notes to G (-5)—an open string. The other three strings of the chord are just the same as in a plain, old-fashioned Db7.

Practice by playing these variations on the 7ths you've been playing a lot. Listen to how the sounds of these chords change when you change one note just this much. Subtle but interesting, no?

Remember, sometimes these chords have the notations # or b instead of + or -, so you might see C7#5 or C7+5. They mean the same thing.

There are other chord varieties we can't possibly cover in this short course: they might be infinite in number. Some of them are the Cm-9, Cm7-5, Cm9, and so on. If you understand the previous discussion of the Ninths and these plus-and-minus 5ths, you can probably figure a lot of them out. You'll have chances to play some raised and lowered 5ths in "Poor Butterfly" and "St. Louis Blues."

The important thing is to give it a try. Most of the time, if it doesn't sound right to you or fit your personal style, you can just play the "regular" 7th. What's a composer going to do—confiscate your capo?

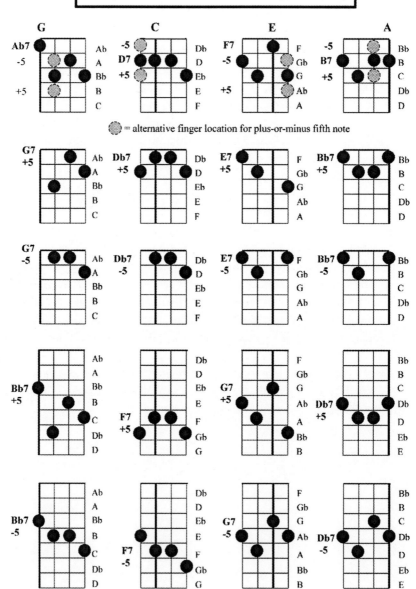

Seventh chords with + or − Fifths (7#5 or 7b5)

Poor Butterfly

Words by JOHN L. GOLDEN
Music by RAYMOND HUBBELL

Arranged by Calvin Chin

St. Louis Blues

W.C. HANDY

Arranged by Calvin Chin

St. Louis Blues (conclusion)

Interlude

A brief lesson in music fundamentals

In the first part of this book, you learned about the "shapes" of chords that you can play on each string. It's amazing but true that when you learned about 50 shapes (for 12 basic chords, 16 advanced, 4 Majors, diminished and augmented, and some 7ths with + and − variations) you discovered how to play almost every chord you'll need.

I hope that opened your eyes to a whole new world of possibilities. For one thing, you'll never be limited to playing just the songs that a music publisher chooses to embellish with chord tablatures.

But what I'm going to teach you in Part 2 is how to play more of the melody in your songs. That means you'll be picking individual notes out of chords and plucking them when they carry the melody. And it means that you need to know where to find each note on the fret board.

Here's what I mean, starting with the A string at the top:

Bb	B	C	Db	D	Eb	E	F	Gb	G	Ab	A		A string
F	Gb	G	Ab	A	Bb	B	C	Db	D	Eb	E		E string
Db	D	Eb	E	F	Gb	G	Ab	A	Bb	B	C		C string
Ab	A	Bb	B	C	Db	D	Eb	E	F	Gb	G		G string

Figure 1

The representation of the ukulele keyboard in Figure 1 shows the note progression along each string, known as the chromatic scale. The 12th fret on each string is one octave higher than the "open" note on that string.

As I hope you've learned by now, when you're playing and need to know where a particular note is located on a string, you can always count through the alphabet range A through G from the open note (never forgetting the "rule of none"!). As you practice more, though, knowing what note you'll play at each and every fret will eventually become second nature to you.

So, Figure 1 shows you how the scales fit on the four strings of the uke. But you also need to know how to identify notes on a score. For simplicity, Figure 2 (on Interlude page iv) shows how the basic notes (no sharps or flats) appear for a 1-1/2 octave range.

You'd play the lowest note in this scale, a low C, by plucking the open C-string. You might play the highest note, a high A, by plucking the 12th fret of the A-string. The more you practice and play, the sooner your brain will be able to "translate" between where the notes are on the keyboard, and where they are on the music score. Eventually, if all goes well, you won't even have to think about the particular fret and string that will turn the score-notes into the tones you want.

Of course, real scores show intermediate tones (sharps, flats, and naturals). Playing a sharp on the uke means that you raise the pitch of a note by a fret; a flat means that you lower the pitch by a fret; and a "natural" reverts to the basic pitch of the note. As you probably know, one note's sharp is another note's flat. So, an Eb is exactly the same as a D#. I've just tried to keep it simple in this book by designating every intermediate note as a flat. You will encounter the sharp (#) symbol sometimes in the cruel outside world, though.

In addition to any sharp, flat, and natural signs in the body of the score, there's also the "key signature" which usually applies to all measures. Frequently, you'll come across a key change in a song, and when that happens you'll follow *that* signature as long as it's in effect.

The opening key signature appears next to the clef symbol at the left end of every line of music. Sharps or flats in the signature show the notes that must be raised or lowered until another symbol appears next to an individual note.

When the key is C there's no signature, simply because the C scale has no sharps or flats. All the other keys contain at least one sharp or flat.

Figure 3 shows an example of how the key signature dictates the pitch of notes in three measures. This short passage is in the key of Eb. In the Eb scale, the A, the B, and the E notes are flatted. So the Eb signature has flats on the B line and on the A and E spaces.

Notice, in the second measure, that the 1st B-note has a natural sign in front of it. That means you ignore the Bb in the key signature. The natural over-rides the key signature every time that note appears in the same measure. In the 3rd measure, however, there's no natural sign, so the pitch of every B will be according to the key signature. You could say that music has three main elements—melody, harmony, and rhythm. You'll be learning how to play melodies on the uke in Part II of this book. You already learned about harmony w hen you started understanding more about chords. Right here I'll mention a few things about rhythm, in which timing and the beat are all-important.

In the short piece of music in Figure 3, there's a ¾ time signature right after the key signature. It means that there are three quarter-notes in each measure. And it means that each measure has three beats. This particular tempo is called "waltz time."

Other popular time signatures are 2/4, 4/4, 6/8, and so on. But the most popular one, especially for the uke, is probably 4/4 (called "fox trot" time), meaning that there are four beats to the measure. Beats can be divided up many ways, with notes that signify the their duration. See Figure 4 to see how notes "tell the time."

So, the beat is dictated by the time signature, the appearance of notes, and other notations. A dot next to a note means that note's duration is increased by 50%. So a dotted half-note is 3 beats instead of 2.

There's another symbol you've already seen in several practice songs: the curved arc that connects some notes. Go back and check out "Smiles" in Lesson 7. These curved lines just mean to hold the notes they connect. you can't really *hold* a note on the uke—not like you can with your voice or on a wind instrument. But in"Smiles," if the arc connects a whole note and a quarter-note, as in the first line of the song, you'd sing it for 5 beats: "Smiles [5 beats] that [1] make [1] us [1] hap [2] py [4]…"

The different beats have varying duration; i.e., the length of time the note is played or sung. The shorter the duration, the faster we say the note is. So a quarter-note is faster than a half-note. I've just shown a series of notes to the 16th. Until you become quite accomplished, it's unlikely that you'll play any faster than that.

Figure 5 shows you different durations for rests, and how these intervals of silence and notes go together to fill the appropriate number of beats in each measure. Remember, this is 4/4 time, as you count the beats.

Finally, I just want to show you a couple of common symbols that tell you exactly where to go back and replay parts of songs, so that the arrangers don't have to keep writing duplicate passages. They're in Figure 6.

And now, we'll move onward to learn some really interesting stuff!

Figure 2

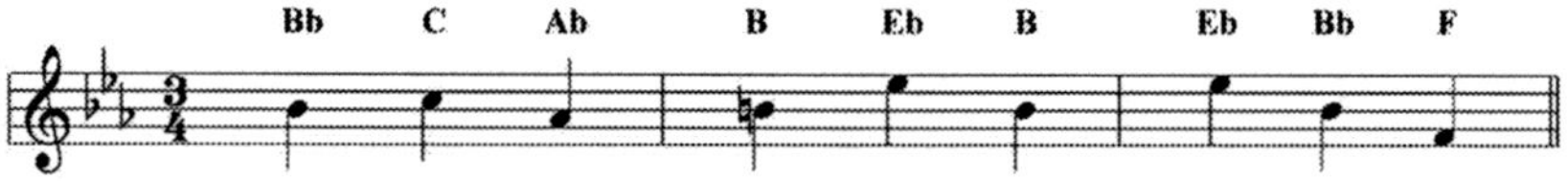

Figure 3

Figure 4

Figure 5

Figure 6

INTRODUCTION TO PART II: STRUMMING MELODIES

Funny thing about playing the ukulele. Even after you've been at it for a while and can play a few songs fairly well, you don't think of it as a possible solo instrument. Most of the time, you're accompanying somebody who's singing, probably yourself.

With most sheet music, the chord changes in the song aren't frequent enough to play much of a melody. The voice does that. Your uke accompaniment is really just laying down the rhythm and some tonal back-up for the notes you sing. But to think along those lines can be pretty limiting—and can limit *you*. That's not as good as it can be!

You know, if you want to take the time to work it out, you can change chords as often as the harmony note changes. No more playing the same sound for two or three bars. And when you can play a whole melody of chords, you've got yourself a potential solo instrument. If your voice isn't too hot, your friends'll probably thank you for developing this skill.

The aim of these next few lessons is to show you how to learn melody strumming and picking, so you'll be able to expand your musical horizons.

With melody strumming, the more chords you know, the better you'll play. You also need to know your fretboard cold—where every note is. When you can instantly find a convenient D chord, for example, to advance the harmony, you'll also be able to pick individual notes—a nice touch.

The best thing about this ability is that it lets you add your own creativity to any song. You can put in whatever embellishments you want—often just moving one finger or by just sliding up and down the fretboard.

When your rendition of the song sounds good to you, then you can write in your additional chords and variations so that other players will be able to play and enjoy your arrangement.

The first time I heard melody strumming was 'way back, more than 70 years ago. A Hawaiian schoolmate played several songs by strumming and picking every note of the melodies. It took me a while to realize how much preparation it had taken him to do this—to find each chord and then, perhaps, to modify it by playing just one or two of its notes, or by adding another note altogether.

Later, I took up piano, organ, and guitar during different stages of my life. While learning the piano and organ, I got a different perspective on the composition of chords. Then I used my insights with my first instrument, categorizing ukulele chords into sets by their root string, and developing a comprehensive chord system. This system was described in detail in the first 11 chapters.

And now, by knowing the way chords are constructed (see Appendix A), we can actually transcribe any sheet music to a ukulele score. Talk about expanding your repertoire!

The process of transcribing sheet music arranged for another instrument to ukulele is simply using the chords and musical notes from the original, and then modifying them for precise sound and effect, and for high or low pitch, to get the variations that appeal to *you*. I'll cover some conventions that will help you do this.

What is modification?

You can modify chords in many ways. By the way, if you don't have your uke handy right now, go and get it. You'll learn more if you actually do these things as you read about them.

Let's get specific. Here's a simple modification that involves adding a note to a "standard" chord. The chord F(C) represents the F major with a C-note included. Play an F major based on the E-string. Then include a C on the A-string, using your pinkie. As you can hear, the change produces a slightly higher tone. By two notes.

Or, you can modify a chord by dropping a note. Example: you can change a Ab dim to an E7, just by playing the E-string open.

Another kind of modification is the chord inversion. For example, you can play a D minor (based on the A string) two ways, but one has more emphasis on the D; the other on the A. Look at the chord inversion examples in the Appendix. Then play the C both ways and listen to the difference.

Inversions are good for you!

Inversions generally involve just the majors, minors, which have only 3 different notes—and augmented chords. But since the uke has four strings, you have the option of choosing any note on either of the duplicate-note strings—just as long as your finger can reach it. For example, the lowest D major includes D, Gb, A, and another A (played with the A-string open). But the inversion of this chord produces a higher tone and emphasizes the D instead of a second A. This change also produces a higher tone.

Other kinds of modifications include suspended notes, as in the sus4 chords. Some examples are shown in Appendix C. And don't forget the 7th +/-5 chords (explained in the last lesson), which let you keep the basic chord sound while adding either of two other notes.

Finally, as you learned in the first part of this book, you can change the pitch of a chord by changing its root string. To reinforce this point, play the A7 based on the A-string, and then that same chord on each of the other three.

Yo-yo's and waggles

These aren't very dignified names, and they'll probably never be heard inside the walls of any respectable music conservatory, but they're useful techniques when you want to play a few measures of repetitive melody.

What I call yo-yoing is simply sliding up and down one or two frets, as, for example, when you alternate between D7 and Db7.

Waggling is best illustrated by moving between, say, D7 and D9. Try it—basing your chords on the C-string. I think you'll see what I mean as you press and lift a single finger on each stroke.

You'll be pleased at how many times these techniques give you the effect you're looking for, and the variety you get when you don't just keep playing the same form of a chord.

How does this look on paper?

In the practice songs ahead, I'll use these notations to indicate when you should play a chord with a higher pitch, and when you should add a note to a "regular" chord:

Remember, you can play any chord at four different places on the fretboard—four different pitches—depending on the root string. Each pitch level above the lowest possible one will have a line below the chord name. So, to take A7 as an example, a simple A7 would tell you to play that chord at the lowest pitch possible—based on the A-string. The next pitch up would be shown as A7, with a single line under the chord name, indicating that you should play the chord at its next higher pitch, in other words, based on the G-string. A7 with a double underline would tell you to use the E-string shape, and, as you'd expect, A7 with a triple underline tells you to play the highest version, based on the C-string.

These notations aren't hard and fast—you might play an inversion which has a pitch somewhere between. Be guided by the melody. Does the pitch at which you play the chord fit the pitch the melody calls for? You be the judge!

As for the parentheses enclosing a note name, you just add that note to the chord. Remember the example I used earlier: F(C) means to play the lowest pitch F major—*and* add a C.

Playing by the numbers

The basic mathematics of music helps you understand the relationships of notes to each other as they form different chords. The cycle of seven full notes, from A through G, is repeated through the whole range of notes playable on the uke, and the 8th note of any scale is the same as that scale's "key," or starting note.

Take a minute to look over the first chart in the Appendix. Underneath the scales I've summarized the "formulas" of chords (e.g., 1-3-5) in their simplest form to help you see how they're put together.

LESSON 13: PUTTING IT TO MUSIC

Well, it's time to stop reading for a while and to start playing.

To get started, I think the best way of showing you the "secrets" of transcribing music scored for other instruments, is to talk you through a bunch of songs. They'll be fun for you to sing and play as you learn!

Later on, feel free to write in your own chords to make the songs more melodic. If you can get to where you play a different chord for each note, you've achieved the valuable skill of making the uke a solo instrument. (Your friends and family might even be *happy* if you didn't always sing!) So, for the first couple of songs, just get the feel of playing a chord for every note on the second chorus. That's the start of the finesse I mentioned a couple of paragraphs back.

A few things to remember, before we do any analysis. If you play a "standard" chord and it doesn't produce the exact sound you're looking for, you can modify it by adding a note. Or by deleting a note or two. Or, you can play it rooted on a different string, moving up or down the fretboard to change its pitch.

Now, it's time to put some of these ideas to music, so to speak. I've made some brief comments about playing the songs, as follows:

The World is Waiting for the Sunrise This score of "Sunrise" is very simple, as you see. As is usually the case with ukulele scores, it has just the treble stave and the melodic notes. If it were a full piano score you'd see a lot more notes, of course. But as you learn transcription skills, you probably should work with just the top notes.

The song was relatively easy to rearrange. Using the chord system I've been talking about from the beginning, we've got almost all the chords you'll need.

Now, this might take a little review. I want you to play the inversion version for G+ and Gm. The purpose is to put emphasis on the G note.

Remember the pitch notation I'm using (one or more lines under the chord name). When there isn't any line, you just play the chord at its lowest. And that would be illustrated by the E7 in the first chorus. Play it based on the E-string.

In bars 5 and 13 of the second chorus, there are two <u>E7</u>s. Play the first one rooted on the A-string, so you can include a high E. The point of this is to capture the fall from a high E to a high D, as the musical notes indicate. A plain E7 doesn't give you this nuance.

Play the second <u>E7</u> rooted on the C-string, so you can reach a higher D.

Letters in parentheses indicate that you'll add the designated note—substituting for another note, of course—to the primary chord. Example: the F(C) in measures 6 and 14. Since the original F already includes a C, you'll emphasize that note by putting it in the chord twice. Just play a regular F chord while you press the A-string C with your pinkie.

In all the songs from here to the end of the book I numbered the chord lines 1 and 2. That means I want you to play *and* sing the top line of chords the first time through. Then just strum the second chorus (#2), playing the bottom line of chords.

Well…with all that out of the way, try playing "The World Is Waiting For The Sunrise." It's a great, happy old tune! Then, come back here and read about the next song…

JA-DA The way you do this song I call "playing by the numbers." As you saw in "Sunrise," some of the chords are underlined, meaning that you should play them at higher pitch. And the parentheses designate a note to be added to the normal chord shape.

At the end of the 7th bar, you'll add an A-flat to the G7 chord. Another example, at various places in the second chorus, is the F(C).

Let me go back to that G7(Ab). When you form the G7 rooted on the G and then add an Ab (the -9 note of the G scale), you've got your fingers in place to play diminished chords, including Abdim and Bdim. I could just as well have used either of those chord names, but I wanted to keep it simpler in these cases, where—as in bars 3, 7, and 13—you're toggling back and forth between G9 and G7.

I don't want to beat this subject to death, but just to remind you of the many different ways to designate chords, I'll mention another possibility. The G7(Ab) could also have been written G7-9. Remember, a "7-9" is the same as a diminished chord.

Chords with numbers not inside parentheses are supposed to be primary (or "standard") chords. But when you see a number without a chord name, as in the 3rd bar, it refers to the previous primary chord. So here, the phrase G9 7 9 7 tells you to alternate between G9 and G7. This notation reduces overcrowding, especially in measures that contain lots of notes (and, in a way, illustrates the notion of "playing by the numbers.")

One more comment: The <u>D</u> you'll find in measures 2, 6, and 14 is a good place for an inversion, and lets you capture the drop from the D to the A. Check the inversion examples in Appendix B.

And now it's time for you to play JA-DA, a great old Dixieland song written long ago, and excellent for ukulele soloing.

The World Is Waiting for the Sunrise

Words by GENE LOCKHART
Music by ERNEST SEITZ

Arranged by Calvin Chin

JA-DA

By BOB CARLETON

Arranged by Calvin Chin

Gypsy Love Song With this song, you'll explore the versatility of inversions.

Now, look at the D major in the 7th bar. When you play it rooted on the C-string, it sounds OK. But what if you wanted to emphasize the sound of the A-note because that happens to be the note in the score? You can apply the inverted shape just by lifting your pinkie to expose the open A note. Your modified chord will now contain two A's. That's another example of the versatility *you* can put into uke chords, because now you've got the notes you want—with equal emphasis.

Here's another example of a modified chord: the last note in the 3rd bar. Remember, a parenthetical letter relates to the previous chord. In this case, we're looking for a G7 with an E added. The note on the music staff is a high E. Because of the underline notation you'll play the G7 rooted on the E string. But now you've eliminated the E note from the chord. If you do want to hear that high E, just slide your pinkie down the fretboard, to the seventh fret on the A-string. Incidentally, only major, minor, and augmented chords can be inverted.

This kind of modification is really useful when you play a song which has very few chords designated for you—in which you might be tempted to keep strumming the same chord for two, or three, or even more bars. And there are no helpful notes in parenthesis—(a), (e), and so forth—to guide you. But here's a powerful principle: the more different chords you play, the better you'll play the melody.

As you begin to master the techniques I'm telling you about, you'll be able to see more places where you can modify chords. For example, the next-to-last note in the third bar is a high D. You're already pressing the A-string D as part of the G7 chord. Emphasize that note by being sure to pick it, maybe even by strumming on only the C-E-A or E-A strings. With this emphasis, you'll capture the rising sound in the score—and play a chord for every note in the bar. Look for these opportunities whenever the arranger hasn't provided a chord to sound note changes.

Gypsy Love Song
(Second version)

By VICTOR HERBERT

Slum - ber on, my lit - tle gyp - sy sweet - heart, Dream of the field and the grove, —

Can you hear me, hear me in that dream - land, Where your fan - cies rove?

Slum - ber on, my lit - tle gyp - sy sweet - heart, Wild lit - tle wood - land dove,

Can you hear the song that tells you All my heart's true love? —

Arranged by Calvin Chin

Arpeggios

At this point, let me mention a great way to carry a melody. It's the *arpeggio* style. With arpeggios, you pick individual notes from the last chord indicated. Here's an example. Look at the <u>E7</u> at the beginning of the 9th bar. You're playing this chord based on the A-string, right? So your B is on the E-string. You can emphasize the B for the last 3 notes of the bar by including that note on the E-string, or you can just pluck the E string. Try it!

I'll indicate good places for arpeggio playing by inserting a wavy line just before the chord name. Your job is to pluck the individual notes in the score. This is made easier because these notes are in the chord following the wavy line.

Look at the 10th bar, which has four unmarked notes between the <u>A9</u> and the A. Why not put them into your song? In this case, you're starting the bar with the A9 rooted on the G-string. So your chord contains B, E, G, AND Db. Since you're already "on" these notes, you can just pluck, in turn, Db, B, E, B—before you play the A chord.

In all the songs to come, pay close attention to unmarked notes. They're probably easy to pick, and the melody will be easier to hear.

If you've followed all that, the next three songs will give you some good practice. I have just a few short comments about them:

Give My Regards to Broadway This one is pretty straightforward. Remember, Line 1 is for playing and singing. Line 2 is for strumming only.

Darktown Strutters' Ball This one calls for just one chorus of melody strumming.

Some of These Days The tempo is significant—don't hurry on this one.

When you've played and practiced all six songs in this lesson, you've worked with the essence of chord shapes (regular and inverted) and their root strings. And you've learned how much variety *you* can add to songs, just by using just a few simple techniques.

Give My Regards to Broadway
(Second version)

GEORGE M. COHAN

Arranged by Calvin Chin

The Darktown Strutters' Ball

Words and music by
SHELTON BROOKS

Arranged by Calvin Chin

Some of these Days
(Second version)

By SHELTON BROOKS

Arranged by Calvin Chin

LESSON 14: The Exotic Major Sevens

A Pretty Girl is Like A Melody Here are a couple of words you'll *never* hear in any prestigious Conservatory of Music: *waggling* and *yo-yoing*. But...they're techniques that can help you really streamline some chord changes.

This song involves a technique I call "waggling," to describe changing from one chord to another, just by lifting a finger.

The major seven (M7) in this song is a good example. Check out what I mean in measure 26, with the chord sequence GM7, G6, M7. You play these rooted on the C-string (so you can get the second higher tones). The neat thing is that you can change back and forth between these chords just by moving one finger. This is the kind of note sequence I look for, because it lets me make easy, fast chord changes.

When you form the GM7, there's an insanely easy way to change to the G6—on the fret under your ring finger. Simply by lifting that finger you've got the G6. Then, to "waggle" back to the M7 all you have to do is press the G with your ring finger again.

So, waggling lets you play alternating chords with your hand in one place on the fretboard.

This song shows how you can waggle fast changes between 7ths and 9ths as well. Try it, with the A7 and A9 chords in the 15th measure.

Remember, the positioning you use (determining the pitch by fingering chords up or down the fretboard) should fit the pitch of the note on the score. In the example above, you'd play the high GM7 because the note is high up on the scale. Another thing to consider when deciding where to position your chords is how they relate to each other on the fretboard.

Now, let's turn for a minute to "yo-yoing." This just means moving a short distance up and down the fretboard. An example: measure 11, which contains the chords C, B, and C again. By playing the C and B both rooted on the A-string, you'll instantly see what I mean. You've got the same situation in measure 25, with Am, Abm, and Am.

After You've Gone In the second measure the alternating F6 and M7 chords call for waggling, and you play the sequence of Dm and Dbm's in measure 14 by yo-yoing. I think you've got the idea by now.

One thing to be aware of, though, is that you might start playing series of chords by yo-yoing and waggling faster than you should, just because the changes are so easy. So, remember the song's tempo and keep the beat consistent!

How Ya Gonna Keep 'Em Down On the Farm This wonderful old World War I vaudeville tune gives you practice with waggling, positioning (to get the pitch that's indicated by the position of the note, high or low), and yo-yoing. It should be real easy for you!

A Pretty Girl Is Like A Melody

Arranged by Calvin Chin

After You've Gone

By CREAMER & LAYTON

After you've gone ___ and left me cry-ing, Af-ter you've gone ___ There's no de-ny-ing;

you'll feel blue, ___ you'll feel sad, ___ You'll miss the dear-est pal you've ev-er had; ___

There'll come a time, ___ now don't for-get it, There'll come a time, ___ when you'll re-gret it;

Some day, when you grow lone ___ ly; Your heart will break like mine and you'll want me on-ly;

Af - ter you've gone, ___ Af-ter you've gone a - way. _____

Arranged by Calvin Chin

How 'Ya Gonna Keep 'Em Down on the Farm After They've Seen Paree?

Words by LEWIS & YOUNG
Music by WALTER DONALDSON

Arranged by Calvin Chin

LESSON 15: Inversions and Refinements

Smiles Here's a chance for a little "inversion practice." In the 15th measure, play the Gbm rooted on the E-string, using its inverted fingering. (Look at the chord inversions in Appendix B if you need a reminder). This'll give you two A notes, and an easier transition to the other chords that follow.

Indiana This is another relatively easy piece, which should present few problems. By this time, I hope that you're able to solve the mystery of most of these songs.

I'm Always Chasing Rainbows In this song, you'll be doing some yo-yoing to make some changes the easy way. Check the passage in the 17th measure—with alternating F7's and G9's. The first position of these chords is the best to use to yo-yo back and forth. You'll find another good place for this technique in the 21st measure (D7's and Db7's) and again in the 29th measure, where you'll find a series of Gm's and Gbm's. It'll be easier for you to play this last passage using the inversions of these chords.

A comment about notation. You'll notice that in these song transcriptions I sometimes use different ways to refer to the same chord. This isn't meant to confuse you, but to show you examples of different ways that composers use to designate chords. The last chord in the 24th measure is shown as "C7-9." This is the same as a G diminished. C7-9 means a C7 plus a flatted ninth note (which, when counting "by the numbers" is a Db) But now, here's what you may not know: a "-9" in a 7th chord is always a diminished chord. So the C7-9 we're talking about here is made up out of a G, a Db (the flatted ninth), an E, and a Bb. In other words, a diminished Db.

I Wonder Who's Kissing Her Now In this song the occasional D̲(d) means that you'll play the inversion of D, in order to get the sound of the extra D on the A-string. As always when you experiment with inversions be aware of the subtle sound difference between the two forms of the same chord.

Pay special attention to the arpeggio notation in the score, from the 2nd measure onward. It's the vertical wavy line preceding the chord name. This signals "arpeggio," and it means that you'll be able to keep to the melody of the song without changing your chord fingering. At least until the next chord. You do this by picking the individual notes out of the chord to match the notes in the score. In the first instance, that will be A, D, and A, as your holding them in the inverted D chord. Then, in Measures 4, 5, and 6, you can play the G chord, then a G note, then a B and then another G. And so on. No more monotonous passages where you just strum the same chord

You'll be seeing lots of arpeggios from here on. When you get comfortable playing this way you might want to go back and make some notations of your own, of the earlier songs in this book. Just start by looking for phrases of two or more notes that you've been playing with the same chord. Put more variety and melody in your renditions!

Smiles
(Second version)

Words by J. WILL CALLAHAN
Music by LEE S. ROBERTS

Arranged by Calvin Chin

Indiana
(Second version)

Words by BALLARD MACDONALD
Music by JAMES F. HANLEY

Arranged by Calvin Chin

I'm Always Chasing Rainbows
(Second version)

Music by HARRY CARROLL
Lyrics by JOSEPH McCARTHY

Arranged by Calvin Chin

I Wonder Who's Kissing Her Now
(Second version)

Lyrics by HOUGH & ADAMS
Music by J. HOWARD & H. ORLOB

Arranged by Calvin Chin

Let Me Call You Sweetheart

Words by BETH SLATER WHITSON
Music by LEO FRIEDMAN

Arranged by Calvin Chin

LESSON 16: A Variety of Unusual Songs

Poor Butterfly There's a chord in the first line that might be new to you: the BmM7. To play it, hold the A-string Bm fingering, and then add a M7 or Bb to it, on the G-string. Remember, M7 stands for the next tone lower than the B in this key. The next lower tone from B is, of course, Bb. (Refer to Appendix A)

There are some good passages for waggling, like the D7 D6 D7 D6 in the 3rd measure. In the 10th measure, you can play the inversion of Gbm, up at the neck of the fretboard, and then waggle your ring finger to get the A. There are some other passages good for waggling in this song. Be on the lookout for them. Remember, sometimes when you use chord inversions you can increase the waggling opportunities.

I've just shown one chorus—the melody chords—for this song. Try singing it with those chords, as well.

Indian Summer Practice playing this song using the "guitar stroke." This lets you emphasize both the chord sound and the melodic note at the same time.

For example, you can play the G in the 1st measure by first striking the B, and then strum across the other strings guitar-fashion. Do it again in the next couple of measures, to catch the change from Gb7 to Bm. Do it again at the beginning of the second line, on the Am and Am7 chords.

In the 11th measure, a guitar stroke is perfect for the Em(g). Play it rooted on the C-string. You've got a two-G-note Em.

For the rest of this song, positioning is very important. Look for the high GM7 and A9. Play the GM7 rooted on the C, and A9 rooted on the E.

Come Back to Sorrento This score includes another notation to tell you to add a required note to a given chord. You've seen lots of parenthetical notations, like F(c), but here I use such suspend chords, as "A7sus4" or "s4". That means you're to suspend the third note but replace it with the fourth. To understand this well, it will help you to refer to Appendix C. In the A7 example, the third note is (db). Replace it with the fourth, a (d), and keep the rest of the A7 intact.

In the 19th measure, finger the E-string A7 but slide your middle finger to (d) on the s4 chord, then waggle back to (db). This notation is exactly like the parenthesis, as in Bm7(g) in measure 13. Composers use both methods, so you should know that mean the same thing.

Remember, there are many ways to provide a given tone—the modification technique, the added note by parenthesis, the 7+/-5, the extended chords, and now, the suspended chords. As long as you finger the major portion of the required chord along with the additions or changes, well—you're in business!

St. Louis Blues Tempo is important in this piece, but the syncopation *you* provide, using your own creativity, can really make your talents shine. The song is pretty easy, until you get to the 40th measure. Here, in order to keep the right rhythm, you've got to use an easy way to make your chord changes. For example, *slide* your finger to make the changes between G and Gb, using the E-string to root those chords.

The Gb to the vibrato G is repeated several times. To get your timing right, go over this passage repeatedly, until you've captured its essence. You'll find that it's very playable when you pick out the individual notes as called for.

I've only written only one chorus for this song, but, with enough practice, you should be able to sing the lyrics to accompany the melody.

Because Play this song slowly, and with feeling. It's a straightforward piece. Use care as you play the chords with notes in parentheses. And pay special attention to the positioning of notes as you play the fifth line, all the way from The Gb+ to the F7. Use the note positions as your guide.

Ave Maria Bet you never thought you'd be playing a timeless hymn on the ukulele! I've included it to prove that the range of music open to you now is really limitless! You should be able to play *anything* from blues to classical compositions—and add your own modifications and personal touches to every song.

Pay special attention to where you position your chords, and be guided by the pitch of the notes in the score. Remember, by "positioning" I'm referring to decisions about which string to use for the root of each chord, so that you can include the specific note, high or low, that's in the written music.

Let's look at some examples. In measure 5 we find a <u>Dm</u> chord that includes a high D. So, the best choice would be the Dm based on the A-string, wouldn't it?

Now, in measure 9, there's another <u>Dm</u>, but this one includes a high F rooted on the G-string.

The last example I'll give you is the <u>Gm</u> in measure 13, which, the score tells us, must include a high D. And that would be the chord rooted on the E-string.

Finally, note the arpeggios in measures 31 and 32. Be sure to pluck the individual notes that are in the score. And, with this lovely song, you've got the material to practice and perfect all the lessons in this course.

Even if your practice doesn't result in total perfection, you know things now that can make you a much better, more entertaining uke musician. Enjoy it!

Poor Butterfly
(Second version--instrumental only)

Words by JOHN L. GOLDEN

Music by RAYMOND HUBBELL

Arranged by Calvin Chin

Indian Summer

By VICTOR HERBERT

Arranged by Calvin Chin

Come Back To Sorrento

Arranged by Calvin Chin

St. Louis Blues
(Second Version)

By W.C. HANDY

Arranged by Calvin Chin

St. Louis Blues
(conclusion)

Because
(Second version)

Words by EDWARD TESCHEMACHER
Music by GUY D'HARDELOT

Arranged by Calvin Chin

Ave Maria
(Second version)

BACH - GOUNOD

Arranged by Calvin Chin

Ave Maria
(Conclusion)

GETTING THE BEST OUT OF UKULELE BREAKTHROUGH

That's about it, for this first edition of *Ukulele Breakthrough*! If you followed the plan of all the lessons, you learned how to:

- find the notes on your fretboard (pretty fast, thanks to the RULE OF NONE)

- play at least an octave worth of major, minor, 7th, diminished, and augmented chords on every string

- play dramatic, advanced, and elegant varieties of sevenths: the Major 7ths and the raised or lowered 5th embellishments

- find at least 500 chord positions, without needing tablature diagrams

- modify chords in several ways

- use such strumming techniques as *waggling* and *yo-yoing*, to make fast and smooth chord changes

- play inversions and use other refinements, such as *arpeggios*

- play instrumental song melodies

- become a much more adept and entertaining uke player!

So…if you're still with me, let me congratulate you for accomplishing a lot! You can do even more toward becoming the uke player you've always wanted to be. Of course, that means the P-word: practice.

As long as you're willing to invest your time and effort, I'd suggest this kind of routine for maybe 30 minutes a day:

(1) Review some of the difficult chords you don't use very often that may appear in one of the lesson songs, such as ninths, raised or lowered 7ths, and so on. Take any one of the lesson songs for each practice session.

(2) Play the song using the "one-string serenade" (all chords based on the same string), to sharpen your skill at finding the notes and fingering the correct chord shapes). Then, do the same for the other three strings. You're <u>really</u> going to know the song well! Next time, work on another song.

(3) Then do the same song using all four strings as your chord bases, but only the chords in the "midway range", between the 3rd and 7th (or 4th to 8th) frets.

(4) <u>Once in a while</u>, do a fingering exercise by playing the entire set of each type of chords on each string. Hard work, but well worth it.

(5) Play the song again "free form", playing whatever chords you want. Don't forget to have fun!

Calvin Chin

APPENDIX A

Chords "by the numbers"

KEY		2		3	4		5		6	7b	M7	8		9
C	Db	D	Eb	E	F	Gb	G	Ab	A	Bb	B	C	Db	D
Db	D	Eb	E	F	Gb	G	Ab	A	Bb	B	C	Db	D	Eb
D	Eb	E	F	Gb	G	Ab	A	Bb	B	C	Db	D	Eb	E
Eb	E	F	Gb	G	Ab	A	Bb	B	C	Db	D	Eb	E	F
E	F	Gb	G	Ab	A	Bb	B	C	Db	D	Eb	E	F	Gb
F	Gb	G	Ab	A	Bb	B	C	Db	D	Eb	E	F	Gb	G
Gb	G	Ab	A	Bb	B	C	Db	D	Eb	E	F	Gb	G	Ab
G	Ab	A	Bb	B	C	Db	D	Eb	E	F	Gb	G	Ab	A
Ab	A	Bb	B	C	Db	D	Eb	E	F	Gb	G	Ab	A	Bb
A	Bb	B	C	Db	D	Eb	E	F	Gb	G	Ab	A	Bb	B
Bb	B	C	Db	D	Eb	E	F	Gb	G	Ab	A	Bb	B	C
B	C	Db	D	Eb	E	F	Gb	G	Ab	A	Bb	B	C	Db

HOW COMMON CHORDS ARE FORMED:

Major chords are *triads* of 3 different notes. Because the ukulele has 4 strings, the key note is used twice. Example: The C major chord includes the 1st, 3rd, and 5th note of the C scale—C, E, G, and another C.

Minor chords are also triads, but with the 3rd note flatted. So the Cm includes C, Eb, G, and another C.

7th chords are formed of 4 different notes, with the 7th note flatted. The C7 includes C, E, G, and Bb.

The **Major 7th** is like the 7th, but without the 7th note flatted. The CM7 includes C, E, G, and B.

The **minor 6th** is similar to the basic minor, with the 6th note added. The Cm6 includes C, Eb, G, and A.

The **minor 7th** is also similar to the basic minor, with the flatted 7th added. The Cm7 includes C, Eb, G, and Bb.

The **ninth** is the 7th chord with the 9th note added. The C9 includes D, E, G, and Bb.

Extended chords have a designated note added. So the Cm+4 or Csus4 includes an F (the 4th note of the C scale).

APPENDIX B

Chord Inversion Examples

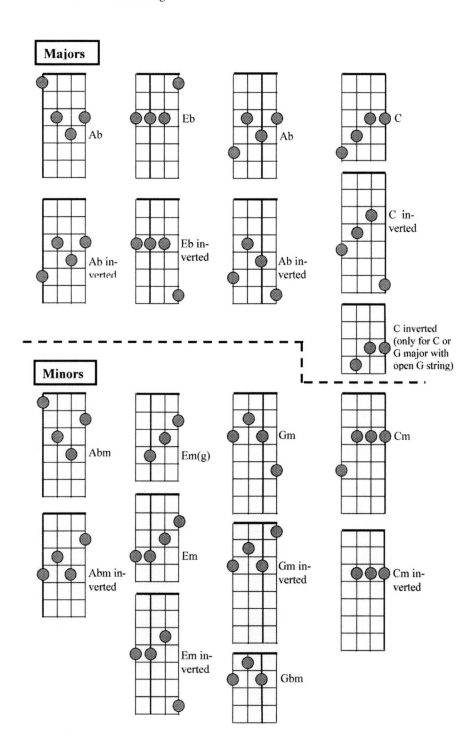

APPENDIX C

Sus4 (Suspended 4th) Chord Examples

The sus4 Rule: Replace the 3rd note of a Seventh chord with the 4th note.

In the examples above...

B7	1 - 3 - 5 - b7 B Eb Gb A	changed to	B7sus4	becomes	1 - 4 - 5 - b7 B E Gb A
F7	1 - 3 - 5 - b7 F A C Eb	changed to	F7sus4	becomes	1 - 4 - 5 - b7 F Bb C Eb
D7	1 - 3 - 5 - b7 D Gb A C	changed to	D7sus4	becomes	1 - 4 - 5 - b7 D G A C
Ab7	1 - 3 - 5 - b7 Ab C Eb Gb	changed to	Ab7sus4	becomes	1 - 4 - 5 - b7 Ab Db Eb Gb

APPENDIX D

Simplified Chord Building

Chords can be divided into two realms—major and minor. Major realm chords may be supplemented by adding, for example, an M7, a flatted 7th, or a 6th note. When you add a flatted 7th to a major chord, you get a 7th. If you add a flatted 7th to a minor chord, you'll produce a Cm7.

Since basic chords (triads) must contain 3 notes of the chromatic scale (1–3–5 for majors; 1–3b–5 for minors), an extra string is available in the 4-string ukulele to let you make them "advanced."

If you focus on the E- and C-string chords, you'll notice that the fingering sometimes looks a bit difficult. But, as you practice more and get better, all these chords are do-able. The point of Appendix D is to show how you can build many different chords out of the basic triad structure. One way to understand the role of the 1–3–5 triad scheme is to remember the numeric composition of these chord types:

Majors 1–3–5–8   Minors 1–3b–5–8

Augmented 1–3–5b–8   Diminished 1–3b–5b–7bb

The following diagrams show how easy it is to produce advanced chords from triads, often just by moving a finger one or two frets:

MAJOR REALM CHORDS

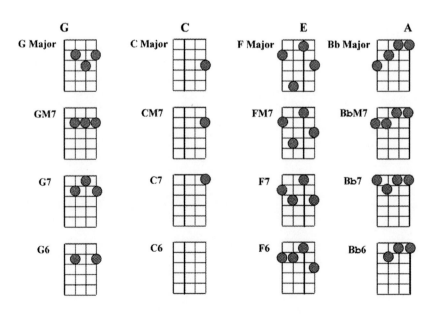

APPENDIX E

Simplified Chord Building, continued

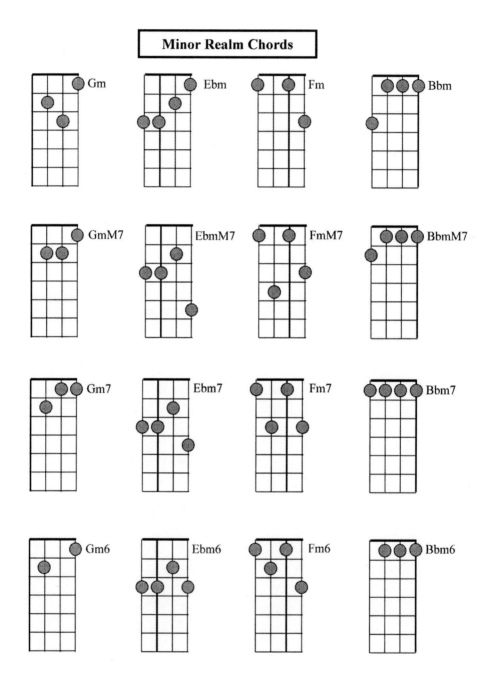

0-595-31258-6

Printed in the United Kingdom
by Lightning Source UK Ltd.
125044UK00001BA/25/A